MISSOURI

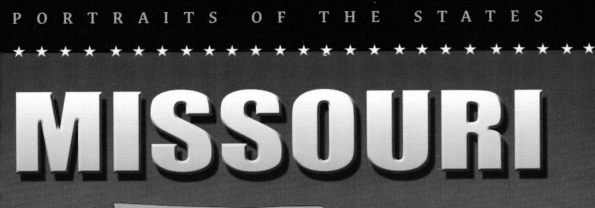

by P. M. Boekhoff

GARETH**STEVENS**
GS
P U B L I S H I
A Member of the WRC Media Family of

Please visit our web site at: www.garethstevens.com
For a free color catalog describing Gareth Stevens Publishing's
list of high-quality books and multimedia programs, call
1-800-542-2595 (USA) or 1-800-387-3178 (Canada).
Gareth Stevens Publishing's fax: (414) 332-3567.

Library of Congress Cataloging-in-Publication Data

Boekhoff, P. M. (Patti Marlene), 1957-
    Missouri / P. M. Boekhoff.
      p. cm. — (Portraits of the states)
    Includes bibliographical references and index.
    ISBN 0-8368-4628-1 (lib. bdg.)
    ISBN 0-8368-4647-8 (softcover)
    1. Missouri—Juvenile literature. I. Title. II. Series.
    F466.3.B64   2005
    977.8—dc22   2005042614

This edition first published in 2006 by
Gareth Stevens Publishing
A Member of the WRC Media Family of Companies
330 West Olive Street, Suite 100
Milwaukee, WI 53212 USA

This edition copyright © 2006 by Gareth Stevens, Inc.

Editorial direction: Mark J. Sachner
Project manager: Jonatha A. Brown
Editor: Betsy Rasmussen
Art direction and design: Tammy West
Picture research: Diane Laska-Swanke
Indexer: Walter Kronenberg
Production: Jessica Morris and Robert Kraus

Picture credits: Cover, p. 17 © CORBIS; pp. 4, 15 Courtesy of Hannibal
Convention & Visitors Bureau; pp. 5, 21 © PhotoDisc; p. 7 © North Wind
Picture Archives; p. 8 © Corel; p. 11 © Eliot Elisofon/Time & Life Pictures/
Getty Images; p. 12 © Bill Greenblatt/Getty Images; pp. 22, 26, 29 © Gibson
Stock Photography; pp. 24, 25 © Library of Congress; p. 27 © Mansell/Time &
Life Pictures/Getty Images; p. 28 © Don Emmert/AFP/Getty Images

Printed in the United States of America

1 2 3 4 5 6 7 8 9 09 08 07 06 05

CONTENTS

★ ★

Words that are defined in the Glossary appear
in **bold** the first time they are used in the text.

On the Cover: The Gateway Arch towers over downtown St. Louis
in Missouri.

Introduction

Missouri is called the "Show-me" state. It has many natural wonders to show. Missouri has two big rivers and many amazing **caves**. Water flowing underground and rivers have carved these caves out of the earth.

In the United States, the West is said to begin at the Mississippi River. Early explorers followed the Mississippi River south to the place where it meets the Missouri River. Explorers could then follow the Missouri River to the West. Because of this, the state is said to be "the **Gateway** to the West."

People take in the sights from a riverboat near Hannibal.

The state flag of Missouri.

MISSOURI FACTS

- Became the 24th State: August 10, 1821
- Population (2004): 5,754,618
- Capital: Jefferson City
- Biggest Cities: Kansas City, St. Louis, Springfield, Independence
- Size: 68,886 square miles (178,415 square kilometers)
- Nickname: The Show-me State
- State Tree: Flowering dogwood
- State Flower: White hawthorn blossom
- State Animal: Mule
- State Bird: Bluebird

5

History

Thousands of years ago, Native Americans came to the area that is now Missouri. They lived mostly along the rivers and streams. They traveled in canoes and caught fish.

The Native Americans hunted in forests. They gathered foods to eat, including pigweed, and planted squash. They built cities on huge mounds of earth. Some of these mounds can still be seen in Missouri.

Trappers and Missionaries

In 1673, the first French came to the area. Jacques Marquette and Louis Jolliet led this group of men. They explored part of the Mississippi River. French fur traders soon followed. They traded with the Native Americans for furs. Christian **missionaries** came, too. They tried to teach their religion to the Native Americans.

Explorers and Settlers

In 1682, the French sent another explorer to the

IN MISSOURI'S HISTORY

Village of the Large Canoes

Missouri is a Native American word. It means "the village of the large canoes." Missouri was the name of a Native village at the meeting place of the Missouri and Mississippi Rivers. The Natives traded with the first French explorers in the village of the large canoes. Today, the place where the Missouri and Mississippi Rivers meet is called St. Louis.

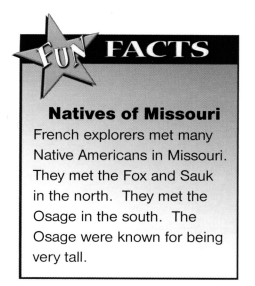
Natives of Missouri

French explorers met many Native Americans in Missouri. They met the Fox and Sauk in the north. They met the Osage in the south. The Osage were known for being very tall.

area. Robert de La Salle explored Missouri and a huge **territory** to the west. He claimed the Natives' land for the French king, Louis XIV. He named the land Louisiana, after the king. In the 1700s, French settlers came to Missouri. They **founded** the towns of Ste. Genevieve and St. Louis.

Robert de La Salle traveled down the Mississippi River and explored the Missouri area for France.

Louisiana Territory

In the late 1700s, Spain held the Louisiana Territory. Then, the French took the land back again. In 1803, they sold the whole territory to the United States.

In 1804, Americans began to explore the area.

Native Americans point to Lewis and Clark's canoes below.

IN MISSOURI'S HISTORY

The Missouri Compromise

In the early 1800s, half of the United States allowed slavery. The other half did not have slavery. Missouri and Maine were not yet states. Missouri had many slaves, and Maine did not have any. To keep the balance even, Missouri and Maine became states at about the same time. Maine joined the nation as a free state, and Missouri came in as a slave state. This deal was called the Missouri **Compromise**.

Meriwether Lewis and William Clark led the way. They saw many wild animals along the rivers. Before long, other explorers came, too. They trapped animals and sold the furs. St. Louis became the home of the Rocky Mountain Fur Company.

U.S. Territory

By 1812, Missouri was a U.S. territory. Its capital was Jefferson City. This city was named for President Thomas Jefferson.

Thousands of European and African settlers lived in Missouri at this time. They set up farms, mines, and animal fur businesses. They moved onto land where Natives had long lived and hunted. As more settlers came, they crowded out the Natives. Natives fought to

keep their land. Over time, diseases brought by the settlers killed many Natives. Others were forced off their land.

Famous People of Missouri

George Washington Carver

Born: About 1865, Diamond Grove, Missouri

Died: January 5, 1943, Tuskegee, Alabama

George Washington Carver's parents were slaves when he was born. He studied for years to learn about plants. He worked at a college. Carver knew that growing one crop for many years wore out the soil. He taught farmers to grow peanuts and soybeans to make the soil rich again. He showed people many ways to use these crops.

The Civil War

By 1861, the leaders of northern states wanted to end slavery. Most of the leaders of southern states wanted to keep slaves to work on big farms. The North and South could not agree. Finally, southern

FUN FACTS

World's Fair

In 1904, the World's Fair was held in St. Louis. It took place one hundred years after Louis and Clark arrived. The fair showed how much the world had changed. New machines, art, and products were on display.

Millions of people came to the fair from all over the world. They came to see new products such as cars and ice cream cones. Both the cars and the cones were big hits with the visitors.

IN MISSOURI'S HISTORY

Kansas City Jazz

In the 1920s and 1930s, a lively new kind of music became popular. It was called jazz. This type of music was first played by African Americans in the United States. It came from a style of music known as blues. In Missouri, Kansas City became a center for jazz. Many musicians went there to perform.

states broke away. They formed their own country. The North wanted to keep all the states in one country. So, the **Civil War** began.

Missouri stayed in the Union. Even so, many people in the state strongly supported the South. The state's leaders certainly did. They refused to send soldiers to fight for the North.

More than one thousand Civil War battles were fought in the state. The war ended in 1865. The South and North were once again a single country. No one was allowed to own slaves in the United States.

War and Depression

In 1917, the United States sent soldiers to Europe to fight in World War I. Missouri farms, mines, and **factories** helped in the war effort. They made supplies for the soldiers.

Many U.S. workers lost their jobs in the **Great Depression** of the 1930s. Wages were very low. Prices paid for crops fell, too. In Missouri, low rainfall and high winds turned the land to dust. People left their farms to search for work. Many could not find jobs.

In the 1940s, the United States went to war again. In Missouri, new factories were opened to make airplanes for

Charlie "Bird" Parker was a great jazz musician who started out in Kansas City in the 1930s.

the war. At last, there were jobs for people who wanted them. This helped the state get out of the Depression.

Missouri in the News

By the early 1980s, **pollution** from factories and huge farms had poisoned the water in Missouri. The

U.S. Senator Jean Carnahan appeared with her family after her husband and son died.

pollution was very bad in a place called Times Beach. It was not safe to live there. Finally, the U.S. government bought the town. Then, it made all the people move.

The government cleaned up the land. It is now being turned into Route 66 State Park. The park has easy, level trails for walking, biking, and riding horses. People are coming back to enjoy the beautiful Meramec River that flows by the park.

2000 Election

During the election of 2000, the state suffered a great loss. Missouri governor Mel Carnahan was running for U.S. senator. Sadly, he and his son were killed in a plane crash three weeks before the election. There was no time to replace him. People still voted for him. He won the election. His wife Jean was chosen to take his place as senator.

★ ★ ★ Time Line ★ ★ ★

1673	Marquette and Jolliet explore the Missouri River.
1682	La Salle claims Missouri for France.
1700s	French settlers come to Missouri.
1803	France sells Missouri to the United States.
1804	Lewis and Clark explore the area.
1821	Missouri becomes the twenty-fourth state.
1861–1865	The United States fights a Civil War.
1904	The World's Fair is held in St. Louis.
1917	U.S. involvement in World War I begins.
1931	Bagnell Dam forms the Lake of the Ozarks.
1941	U.S. involvement in World War II begins.
1965	The Gateway Arch is built in St. Louis.
1983	The U.S. government buys Times Beach and moves people from their homes because of pollution.
2000	Mel Carnahan is elected senator after he dies in a plane crash. His wife is chosen to replace him.

People

A lmost six million people live in Missouri. More than two-thirds of them live in cities. The biggest cities are Kansas City and St. Louis.

There are two cities named Kansas City. They are very close together. One is in Missouri, and the other is in Kansas.

The Mississippi River divides the city of St. Louis. West St. Louis is in Missouri. East St. Louis is in Illinois.

Hispanics: In the 2000 U.S. Census, 2.1 percent of the people living in Missouri called themselves Latino or Hispanic. Most of them or their relatives came from Spanish-speaking backgrounds. They may come from different racial backgrounds.

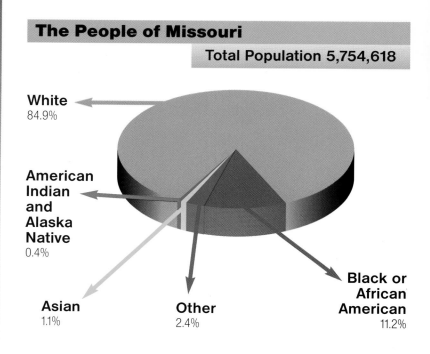

The People of Missouri

Total Population 5,754,618

White
84.9%

American
Indian
and
Alaska
Native
0.4%

Asian
1.1%

Other
2.4%

Black or
African
American
11.2%

Percentages are based on the 2000 Census.

People once used riverboats to travel along the Mississippi. Now most of these boats carry tourists.

Some people in Missouri live on farms. Rich farm-land covers about two-thirds of Missouri. There are thousands of small farms.

Then and Now

Long ago, thousands of Native Americans lived in Missouri. Then, the French and Spanish traders came. Today, few Natives live in Missouri.

By 1820, about seventy thousand people lived in

Famous People of Missouri

Roy Wilkins

Born: August 30, 1901, St. Louis, Missouri

Died: September 8, 1981, New York, New York

Roy Wilkins lived and worked in Kansas City, Missouri. He was an African American. In his time, many people did not treat African Americans fairly. Wilkins knew that was wrong. He stood up for the rights of African Americans. He became a **civil rights** leader. Now, laws protect the rights of all people.

Missouri. The majority of them were settlers. They mostly came from the eastern and southern parts of the United States and from Europe. Even now, most of the people in the state are white.

In 1820, more than ten thousand slaves lived in Missouri. After the Civil War, the slaves were freed. Many stayed in Missouri. Some became farmers. Today, more than 10 percent of the people in Missouri are African Americans.

Just as in the old days, people are still moving to Missouri from other places. Some come from other parts of the country. Others come from faraway places. In 2002, more than eighty-six hundred people moved to Missouri from other parts of the world. Many came from eastern Europe. Others came from Asian countries and Mexico.

Education

Education has always been important to the people of Missouri. An elementary school was started in St. Louis in 1774. In 1873, the first public kindergarten in the country opened in St. Louis. In 1908, the world's first journalism school was started at the University of Missouri.

Religion

Almost 90 percent of people in Missouri are Christian. About 25 percent of these Christians are Baptist. Jews, Muslims, Buddhists, and those who practice Native American religions also live in Missouri.

Kansas City, Missouri, is on the south shore of the Missouri River.

The Land

Missouri is a land of rivers. The two largest rivers in the United States flow through Missouri. The Mississippi flows north to south. The Missouri flows west to east. It flows into the Mississippi. Many smaller rivers and streams flow into these two great rivers.

The Northwestern Plains

Northwestern Missouri is a land of plains. The Osage Plains are north of the Osage River. They are prairies with low, rolling hills. Prairies are covered with grass and flowers but few trees. Today, this land is used to grow grain. The Till Plains are further north. These plains have many streams. The rich soil is **tilled** for growing corn.

Dams and Lakes

Many of the rivers in Missouri have dams. Dams slow a river's flow. The water that can't flow through the dams forms lakes. Missouri has some of the largest of these artificial lakes in the United States.

FUN FACTS

The Mississippi Alluvial Plain

The southeast corner of Missouri is called the Mississippi **Alluvial Plain**. Anything washed away by water is called alluvium. Earth, sand, and rocks that wash up onto land make alluvial soil. A plain is smooth and flat. The Mississippi Alluvial Plain is made of soil washed up by the Mississippi River. Today, cotton, soybeans, and rice grow on this plain.

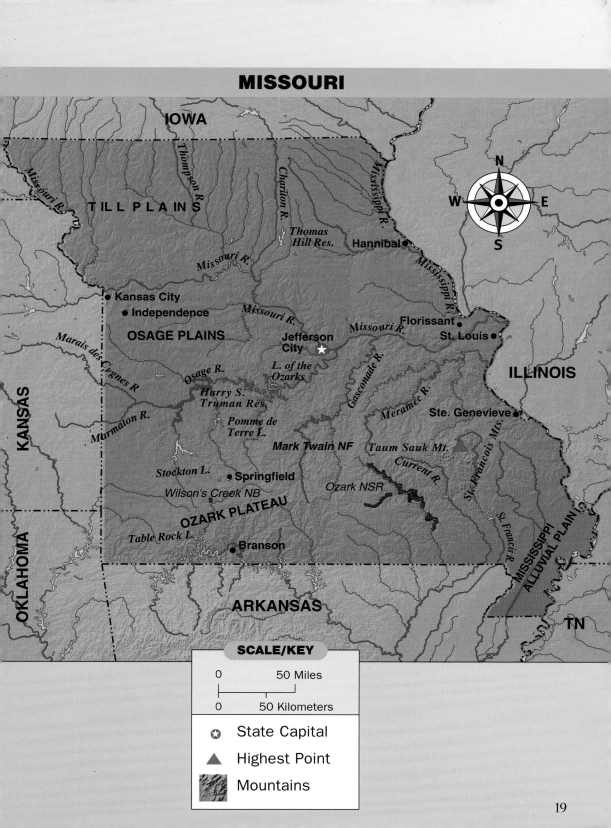

MISSOURI

IOWA

Thompson Rs

Chariton R.

Mississippi R.

T I L L P L A I N S

Missouri R.

Thomas Hill Res.

Hannibal

Mississippi R.

N
W E
S

Kansas City
Independence

OSAGE PLAINS

Missouri R.

Jefferson City

Missouri R.

Florissant
St. Louis

Marais des Cygnes R

Osage R.

L. of the Ozarks

Gasconade R.

ILLINOIS

Harry S. Truman Res.

Pomme de Terre L.

Meramec R.

Ste. Genevieve

Marmaton R.

Mark Twain NF

Taum Sauk Mt.

St. Francois Mts.

Stockton L.

Springfield

Current R.

Ozark NSR

Wilson's Creek NB

OZARK PLATEAU

St. Francis R.

KANSAS

OKLAHOMA

Table Rock L.

Branson

ARKANSAS

MISSISSIPPI ALLUVIAL PLAIN

TN

SCALE/KEY

0   50 Miles

0   50 Kilometers

⭐ State Capital

▲ Highest Point

Mountains

19

People created the largest lake in Missouri. It is called the Harry S. Truman **Reservoir**. Another large artificial lake is Lake of the Ozarks. It was made when the Osage River was slowed by the Bagnell Dam.

Major Rivers

Mississippi River
2,340 miles (3,765 km) long

Missouri River
2,466 miles (3,968 km) long

Osage River
500 miles (805 km) long

FUN FACTS

Earthquakes!

In 1810 and 1811, three big earthquakes shook southeastern Missouri. The shocks were so strong that people living 1,000 miles (1,600 kilometers) away felt them. They may have been the strongest quakes ever to occur in the United States.

The Ozarks

The southwestern part of Missouri is known as the Ozark **Plateau**, or the Ozarks. The Ozark Plateau is the largest part of the state and is full of natural wonders. It has rivers, streams, and springs. It has caves, forests, hills, and small mountains, too.

The Black, James, and St. Francis Rivers are in the Ozark Plateau. They have some of the best fishing spots in Missouri. Another great fishing spot is the Current River. It flows very fast. It is one of Missouri's most beautiful rivers.

Springs and Caves

Many of the rivers in Missouri are made by

springs. Springs are places where water comes up out of the earth. More than ten thousand springs are in the Ozarks. The biggest spring there is called Big Spring.

Missouri's rivers and springs have carved caves underground. These caves are filled with beautiful rock formations. Many caves store fresh spring water.

Animals and Plants

Red foxes live all over Missouri. The foxes eat small animals, nuts, and berries. White-tailed deer, beavers,

muskrats, and skunks make their homes in Missouri as well.

Birds that live in Missouri include blackbirds, purple finches, blue jays, cardinals, orioles, woodpeckers, and mockingbirds. Many kinds of fish swim in Missouri's waterways, including buffalo fish, pike, and bass.

About one-third of Missouri is covered with forests. Oak and hickory are the main trees found there.

Red foxes live in all 114 counties of Missouri.

Economy

About one-third of the people in Missouri work in the service industry. Service workers help people. Some work in restaurants, hotels, stores, and **tourist** attractions. Tourists bring many jobs to Missouri because they eat in restaurants, stay in hotels, buy things in stores, and visit attractions. Others service workers have jobs as police officers, firefighters, doctors, and nurses.

Every year, more than seven million tourists visit Branson to see music shows.

Many workers make goods for sale. They work in factories and offices. Some of them make books. They also build airplanes, railroad cars, boats, and trucks. They make flour, beer, soap, and paint.

Farms

Farming is very important in Missouri. Only 4 percent of the people work on farms, though. The main crop is soybeans. Corn, cotton, and wheat are also big crops. Many Missouri farmers grow apples, peaches, grapes, and vegetables. Some raise hogs, beef cattle, chickens, and turkeys.

Natural Resources

Missouri produces charcoal, lumber, and wood products such as oak flooring. Missouri also leads the country in mining of **lead**.

How Money Is Made in Missouri

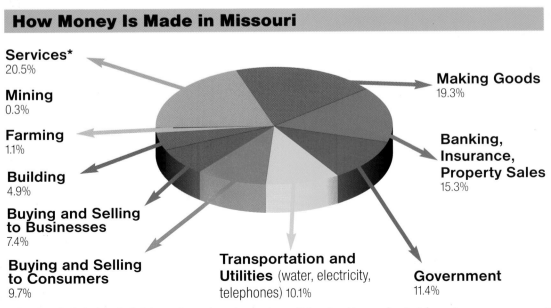

Services*
20.5%

Mining
0.3%

Farming
1.1%

Building
4.9%

Buying and Selling to Businesses
7.4%

Buying and Selling to Consumers
9.7%

Transportation and Utilities (water, electricity, telephones) 10.1%

Government
11.4%

Making Goods
19.3%

Banking, Insurance, Property Sales
15.3%

* Services include jobs in hotels, restaurants, auto repair, medicine, teaching, and entertainment.

Government

Jefferson City is the capital of Missouri. The state's leaders work there. The government has three parts, or branches. They are the executive, legislative, and judicial branches of government.

Executive Branch

The governor is the leader of the executive branch. This branch makes sure that people follow the laws of the state. The lieutenant governor helps the governor. The cabinet is made up of people who work for and help the governor.

Legislative Branch

The legislative branch makes state laws. It is made up of the Senate and the House of

The Missouri State Capitol Building is made from limestone.

Harry S. Truman was born and raised in Missouri. He served as a U.S. Senator from Missouri from 1934 to 1944. In 1945, he became president of the United States.

Representatives. They work together in the General Assembly to make laws.

Judicial Branch

The judicial branch is made up of judges and courts. Judges decide what the laws mean. People who may have broken laws go to court. The courts decide whether or not a person is guilty.

County Governments

Missouri has 114 counties plus one independent city, St. Louis. Each has its own laws and government.

MISSOURI'S STATE GOVERNMENT

Executive		Legislative		Judicial	
Office	**Length of Term**	**Body**	**Length of Term**	**Court**	**Length of Term**
Governor	4 years	Senate (34 members)	4 years	Supreme (7 justices)	12 years
Lieutenant Governor	4 years	House of Representatives (163 members)	2 years	Appeals (32 judges)	12 years

Things to See and Do

People like to come to Missouri to visit the caves and waterways. One of Missouri's largest caves is Marvel Cave. It has 10 miles (16 km) of underground tunnels. Marvel Cave is near Branson, which has forty theaters. Each year, Branson has a festival with crafts and folk music.

Many visitors come to Lake of the Ozarks. This area has show caves. Meremac Caverns is nearby. Every year, the world's only underground bodybuilding contest is

FUN FACTS

Caves

Missouri has more than five thousand caves. About twenty of them are show caves. Show caves are lighted and have paths through them. They have guided tours. Missouri's caves are made from pretty rocks that look like water flowing. The rock forms have names like flowstone, popcorn, and soda straws.

Visitors ride through Fantastic Caverns in Springfield.

Mark Twain

Born: November 3, 1835, Florida, Missouri

Died: April 21, 1910, Redding, Connecticut

Mark Twain's real name was Samuel Clemens. He grew up in Hannibal, Missouri. In *The Adventures of Tom Sawyer* and *The Adventures of Huckleberry Finn*, Mark Twain wrote about what it was like to grow up in Missouri in the 1800s. Steamboats carried people and trade goods on the mighty rivers. Runaway slaves hid in caves.

held in Meremac Caverns. In this contest, strong men and women show off their muscles. It is called the Caveman Classic.

People can visit the cave Mark Twain wrote about in his story *The Adventures of Tom Sawyer*. They can also visit the Mark Twain Home and Museum in Hannibal. Once a year, Hannibal holds a festival called National Tom Sawyer Days.

Other caves of special interest in Missouri include one that is said to have been a hideout for the outlaw Jesse James and one that holds the record for the most underground weddings.

Author Samuel Langhorne Clemens is known as Mark Twain.

Sports

Missouri has many big-league sports teams. Both the St. Louis Cardinals and the Kansas City Royals have players in the Baseball Hall of Fame. In 1985, the two teams met in the World Series. The Royals won.

Football fans in Missouri cheer for the St. Louis Rams or the Kansas City Chiefs. Hockey fans enjoy St. Louis Blues games. Some people like to visit the International Bowling Museum and Hall of Fame in St. Louis.

Jefferson City

Jefferson City is the state capital. The capitol building is made of limestone found in the state. Big paintings on the building's walls show scenes from Missouri's past.

The St. Louis Rams played in the Super Bowl in 2000.

Katy Trail State Park is a hiking and biking path that runs through the area. It is built on an old railroad line. The trail winds along the Missouri River for 225 miles (362 km). People also enjoy swimming, boating, and fishing along Missouri's waterways.

Visitors go fishing on Lake Taneycomo in Branson.

Famous People of Missouri

Maya Angelou

Born: April 4, 1928, St. Louis, Missouri

Poet Maya Angelou's real name is Marguerite Johnson. When she was twelve, she moved to San Francisco with her mother. She changed her name to Maya Angelou when she became a dancer. In 1992, Bill Clinton invited her to read a poem on the day he became president of the United States. She read her poem called "On the Pulse of Morning."

alluvial plain — flat land that has earth, sand, and rocks washed up onto it by water

caves — natural underground rooms and tunnels

civil rights — basic rights of a citizen, such as to vote, go to school, and own property

Civil War — a war between people of the same country — in this case between northern and southern U.S. states

compromise — an agreement made by two groups to settle an argument

factories — buildings where goods and products are made

founded — something started or set in place the first time

gateway — an opening

Great Depression — a time when many people and businesses lost money

journalism — the study of writing news for newspapers, radio, and television

lead — a white metal substance found in nature

missionaries — people sent to spread their religion

plateau — a large, flat area that is higher than the land around it

pollution — waste that makes water, air, or land unclean

reservoir — an artificial lake where water is stored

territory — an area that belongs to a country

tilled — plowed, or broken up, to allow seeds to sink in and grow

tourist — a person who travels for pleasure

Books

I Wonder Why Stalactites Hang Down and Other Questions about Caves. I Wonder Why (series). Jackie Gaff (Kingfisher)

Maria Tallchief: America's Prima Ballerina. Maria Tallchief with Rosemary Wells (Viking)

Missouri Facts and Symbols. The States and Their Symbols (series). Emily McAuliffe (Hilltop Books)

The Missouri River. Rivers of North America (series). Leon Gray (Gareth Stevens)

The Osage. Native Peoples (series). Janet Riehecky (Bridgestone)

Red Foxes. Grassland Animals (series). Patricia J. Murphy (Capstone Press)

Web Sites

MDC Kids! The Missouri Department of Conservation
www.conservation.state.mo.us/kids

Missouri Facts, Map, and State Symbols
www.enchantedlearning.com/usa/states/missouri

Missouri State Parks Kids' Page
www.mostateparks.com/kids.htm

Osage Indians
www.mnsu.edu/emuseum/cultural/northamerica/osage.html

INDEX